Judging for Ourselves:

The Witness of Peter Annett

A One Act Play

by Kevin Annett

The play is set in London, England during the 1760's and the years that follow. The protagonist is Peter Annett, a former clergyman and schoolteacher turned free thinking lecturer and writer. He has been imprisoned by the Attorney-General for having committed "*blasphemous and seditious libel*" in his written criticism of the Church of England and the authenticity of the Bible.

The time is both then and now.

THE

FREE ENQUIRER.

BY

PETER ANNETT.

Prove all things,
St. Paul.

London:
PRINTED AND PUBLISHED BY R. CARLILE, 135, FLEET STREET

1826.

SCENE ONE

Lights up on PETER ANNETT, an aged man with long grey hair and shabby clothes. He sits at a table, center stage. The setting is a dingy prison cell with a table, chair, and cot. Prison bars are on the only window. He reads from a book, then closes it thoughtfully. He stands slowly and gazes out the window and turns to the audience.

PETER

When I was a boy in Liverpool I could stand at the crest of Edgehill and look down at the Mersey shoreline crowded with ships. Many of them were newly returned from unloading their cargos of slaves in Jamaica and America. I remember how I longed to race down the hill to explore those ships, but my father forbade it. He was an Anglican deacon who ran a mission to seamen, and he knew the ways of the waterfront. His ministry prospered from the slave trade, as did all of Liverpool. He told me that God had made the black man to serve the white, quoting from scripture to prove his case. When I asked him where master and slave were in the Garden of Eden, he beat me with his cane until I could not stand.

PETER looks out the window. A distant sound of a bell strikes twice. Peter turns to the table and picks up a pamphlet lovingly. Then he faces the audience.

4

PETER *(reciting)*

"Reason is a divine faculty; it is God within us and incarnate. Why then do we do not judge for ourselves what is true?" *(pause)* Even my father's beatings did not prevent me from asking that. And the blows continued and grew worse the older I became and the more I held to my own judgement. *(pause, angrily)* Did Jesus turn water into wine? Did he issue forth from a virgin? How does common sense judge these presumptuous fairy tales? And yet law and religion forbid such an inquiry! We freeborn Englishmen must dare not question scripture or employ our God given reason lest we be shackled like a Negro in a stinking hole like this one!

Peter holds up the pamphlet angrily.

PETER

Listen to me! My crime has been to write these words: *(reciting)* *"We Free Enquirers shall expose the hidden works of darkness and drive falsity to the bottomless pit. Let all sanctimony and religious enthusiasm depart before the dawn of reason!"* Thus said I, Peter Annett, in this year of our Lord 1761, in the first issue of my publication *The Free Enquirer*.

PETER stares at the audience and extends both his hands.

PETER

And so, as night follows day, my work was proscribed and outlawed by order of the Attorney-General and a judgement of the Court of King's Bench. My writings were declared to be treasonous and a blasphemous libel against the doctrines of Christianity. I was shackled in the public pillory in Charing Cross and pelted with rocks and offal. Then I was sentenced to hard labor here in Bridewell Prison, now, in my seventieth year.

He sets the pamphlet down and steps towards the audience.

PETER

The raised hand of the state and its church is no less severe than that of a father, on earth or in an imagined heaven. Its blow falls on any who question the creeds that sustain their rule. Oh, what a harshly learned lesson has that been! When in my bookish innocence I wrote that all things must be judged according to whether they seem reasonable, how could I have known King George himself would take offense at my words! What was I to think when the high court judge demanded of me whether it was my intent to call into question the monarchy as well as the church's doctrine of the miracles of Christ? Was I the judge of society as well as scripture?

PETER pauses and smiles.

PETER

Indeed I am! One cannot throw a stone at the Church of England and not strike the Crown. Although in truth I never intended the insurgency I am accused of, I understand their fear. It is a poor master who does not detect his ruin in the doubts of his servants.

Pause. Peter gestures at his surroundings.

PETER

When I was first imprisoned in this dank place, I had a visitor, appearing uninvited like one of Job's tormenters. His name was Thomas Sherlock and he came to me to gloat. It was not the most honorable deed of a Bishop of London and a member of the King's Privy Council, but one that befit his character, and lack of it. *(pause)* You see, for years, Sherlock's hired band of thugs pursued me across London, smashing my printing presses and burning my books. It was he who compelled the Attorney General to prosecute and condemn me for publicly challenging his clerical nonsense. *(smiling)* No doubt the venerable Bishop did not take kindly to me calling him a scoundrel and an impotent poltroon in print. But I never mince words with the clergy, or with any dupe monger who claims to speak for an invisible god.

PETER smiles in satisfaction and pulls up the chair and sits.

PETER

Bishop Sherlock and I had never met before. He was much as I imagined him to be, as I was to him, no doubt. He looked about this prison and then at me with an undisguised disdain. *"See how your pride and insolence has brought you here, Master Annett"* exclaimed Sherlock. And I replied, *"Aye Bishop, as yours has brought you to hobnob with Pilate and Herod".* (smiling) My sling could not have struck his Goliath more accurate. Sherlock's fat visage reddened like an abattoir as his sputtering tried unsuccessfully to form itself into words. And so, I continued, *"Do have a seat, Bishop, lest the considerable weight of your office, your frame, and your sins cause you to collapse".* (chuckling) The poltroon did not tarry for long.

PETER smiles in remembrance and then looks tired.

PETER

We are advised to forgive those who persecute us. But Jesus' admonition is not moral instruction. It is quite reasonable advice. For why hate the one throwing the stone when it is placed in his hand by others? Thomas Sherlock was spawned by the Blasphemy Act of 1697, made law by Parliament when I was but an infant!

PETER looks at audience curiously.

PETER

I see you have not heard of this infamy. Then let me explain it. Under that law, which has never been revoked, any Englishman who denies the Trinity or Christ's co-equal status with God is declared to be a public criminal and without a trial is thrown into prison and penury! What a crushing weight has been laid on the free conscience of my countrymen, now and in years to come! Does Jesus himself not say in the twelfth chapter of Luke that we are to judge all things for ourselves? Instead, the England of Thomas Sherlock refutes our Lord with a man-made law that says there is only one worldly judge of matters of thought, and that is the King himself! Hah!

PETER throws up one arm in disgust and walks upstage. He paces as he speaks agitatedly.

PETER

What is a free man to do in the face of abject tyranny? Blithely submit, and crawl about his miserable life like a mule in harness? Such an obtuse ass is what Bishop Sherlock calls a faithful Christian! Then let me be called faithless. I will be free in my thoughts or dead in my traces.

9

PETER begins coughing and gagging violently. After expunging into a handkerchief, he looks up weakly.

PETER

God curse this this blasted consumption! The dampness of this place only worsens it.

Peter pauses, then walks to the window and gazes out thoughtfully.

PETER

It is late. *(He turns to the audience)* You know, a prison cell is the ideal place for a man nearer the end of his years than the beginning. It compels him to remember and to conclude himself.

Pause

PETER *(peacefully)*

I am aware of what led me here and I have no regrets. I see each turn in my road and what I left behind to take another step. And it is all joy to me! But the sweetness of my inner freedom will never be recalled in a history book. Neither can I speak of my substance, despite my literary talents.

Pause as he looks inquiringly at the audience.

PETER

I ask you this. Does it not seem that a great fog of uncertainty clouds our live and our search for final meaning? Does that cloud not threaten to blot out the bright sun of reason? Nonetheless, that faculty is intact. My conscience is clear, and my memories.

PETER returns to the table and sits and stands behind it as if to deliver a lecture.

PETER

More than a century before I drew breath, my Annett ancestors fled from their homes in France to come to these shores. They were Huguenot Protestants, free in their thoughts and devoted to Christ rather than the pope. And for that reason, my people were condemned to die by that royal whore Catherine Medici and her gang of throat-cutting papists. Good Queen Bess gave us sanctuary in this fair land of England, may God preserve her. But Spanish galleons threatened to subjugate our new home, reminding us that no place is safe from religious tyranny. So, even when danger had passed, our family remained exiles, always ready to leave our hearths to preserve our freedom and our conscience. Perhaps that is why I have never felt that I have a home anywhere except in my own thoughts.

PETER stares off reflectively.

PETER

My father expected me to follow him into the ministry. Apprenticed at his side since I was a boy, I saw the leisure time he had to read and compose his homilies, and I welcomed such a life. But I shunned the pomp and presumptions of his Church of England. I chose instead to be ordained with the Non-Conformists. Father never forgave me. My justification to him was as brief as our conversations. I said, "Father, was our Lord one to drink from a golden chalice and preach in rich purple robes?"

PETER smiles and turns to some papers on the table. He searches and finally lifts a sheet.

PETER *(happily)*

I am grateful that the drunken disposition of my jailer allowed this gemstone to miss his inspection. It is a letter sent to me some years ago by the French philosopher Voltaire. He congratulated me on the publishing of my first work, entitled "The Resurrection of Christ Reconsidered". *(smiling)* I am pleased to say that my work gave Bishop Sherlock a particularly hard twist.

Peter chuckles and then reads from the sheet of paper.

PETER

At one point in his letter Voltaire remarks, "Master Annett, I applaud your brilliant exposition of our Deistic principles even as I detect a hard edge and alacrity in your text that comes I suspect from something other than reason. Perhaps like me you have learned from life that our mind is best sharpened against the paternal grinding stone that was resolved to crush us from birth." (*PETER lays the sheet down reverentially.*) My father heard me preach only once, just before he died. He sat unobtrusively in a rear pew among my rude and unwashed parishioners, glaring coldly at me as he always did. But after the service he came to me and his eyes were gentle and tearful. I had never seen him so. (*Pause*) Father bore a remorse that day that would never be spoken. I only heard it later, soon after his death, in the letter he left me in his testament. (*PETER pauses and then speaks with a faltering voice.*) In his testament Father wrote these words: "*The Lord has laid his hand on you Peter, and you will suffer much for righteousness' sake. But His chosen ones who endure the fire will inherit the kingdom denied to the rest of us.*"

PETER bows his head. Lights down.

THE

FREE ENQUIRER.

No. 1.]   SATURDAY.   [Oct. 17, 1761.

If REASON'S *for me, God is for me too.*
CHURCHILL.

AND no wonder; for reason is a divine faculty; it is the divinity operating within us; it is God incarnate; and it is in the army of this Lord of Hosts, that we, the Free Enquirers, enter volunteers to encounter error and imposition, wherever they appear. The weapons of this warfare are not carnal, but spiritual; and will prove mighty in pulling down their strong holds, and in treading Satan under our feet. The light of the Sun of Reason shall dispel all mists or mysteries that obscure its rays; the darkness of ignorance shall flee at its rising. All doctrines founded in error, or fraud, or nursed by fear, shall be confounded by that authority which we are determined to advance above all other authorities; for it is the authority of God. We will bring to light the hidden works of darkness, ransack all nature to find out truth, and drive falsity to the bottomless pit. The whole universe affords us materials. Our title intimates our attention of examining all subjects which can be brought within the cognizance of human reason; *that* alone can bound our field, and limit our inquiries. At the trumpet of Reason, the dead shall be raised. Before that bar, all shall come to judgment: and it shall be known who are, and who are not sinners and saints, infidels and true believers. The veil of the temple, the curtain, the covering of

SCENE TWO

In the darkness there is a sound of shouting, protest, guns firing, screams.

MALE VOICE *(excitedly)*

The food rioting has spread into the city, Colonel. You are ordered to take whatever measures are required to suppress the mob before it reaches Lambeth Palace. They are calling for the hanging of the His Excellency the Archbishop!

SECOND MALE VOICE

But why, your Lordship? Why the Archbishop, for pity's sake?

MALE VOICE

Good God, man! The Church is the biggest landowner in the home counties! And the biggest grain hoarder! Get your troops to Lambeth! If the Church falls, then so do we!

More sounds of rioting, shouts, disorder. Lights up on PETER's cell. He is lying on a cot. The noise continues and he raises his head. Pale reddish light shines through the window. PETER sits up and rubs his face tiredly. He looks to the window and shakes his head sadly.

PETER

My God. The third time this week.

Peter rises slowly and drinks some water from a basin on a side shelf. More shouting is heard and breaking of glass. PETER shouts angrily towards the window.

PETER

Just feed them, you stupid bastards! All they want is bread!

PETER kicks the wall in anger, cursing aloud. He walks to the table and riffles with some papers, then tosses them away in frustration.

PETER *(angrily, to the audience)*

All my words. All my appeals to reason. What do they weigh against the power of evil in this world? Against the oppression of a few over the many? *(angrily)* The same men who condemned me and put me here are ordering their dragoons to fire and hack into those mobs. Mobs? They're starving women and children! Penniless farmers and laborers thrown out of their homes by Bishops and Bankers hungry for their land! I have shared holy communion with those same people who are rioting. I know their faces and their stories. I have sat in their hovels and watch their children die of hunger.

16

PETER looks at the audience pleadingly.

PETER

How often have I heard them ask me so pitiably, *"Pastor, when will Christ return to free us from our hunger? How long should we forgive those who starve and beat us?"* What could I tell them? How could I feed them with lies about assured salvation while their stomachs shrank, and their children died?

Pause

PETER

The truth was, I could do it no longer. I ran out of words. I finally saw – I was made to see by them - who I was, there in my snug pulpit. I was a servant of the Crown. I was licensed by it to laudanum the poor with religion and false promises so they would remain in their place and die quietly. But the lie ended for me, as it had to. I left the church forever in my middle years.

PETER gestures to the window.

PETER

Those people out there are still my congregation. I am ministering to them yet, but on a greater stage. The city of London, indeed the entire world, is my pulpit now.

PETER holds up a large sheet of paper from the table.

PETER *(passionately)*

My sermons are now the broadsheets of my writings that I post on the walls of the east end. I am tearing down the fraud and superstition that chains the minds of the poor. Once their thoughts are free, they cannot but free their lives as well! It surprises me not one whit that I am so hated and attacked by those who profit from their miserable serfdom!

PETER pauses, then seems to grow suddenly weary. He sighs quietly and walks to the table, standing behind it in lecture pose.

PETER

I could find no work after I left the ministry. I had not parted on good terms. Not even the dissenting Christians would tolerate my questioning of scripture. My name became anathema in church circles and thereby everywhere in England. *(pauses reflectively)* For a time, I lived off the meagre inheritance provided by my father, spending my days wandering despondently in the streets of my youth and scribbling what would one day be my first book. But my heart yearned to challenge the lies with more than words! I longed to tear down their putrid Tower of Babel! Thus was I drawn to London, the heart of the beast. Farewell then to Liverpool!

PETER *(pausing and smiling)*

Even as I cast my bread upon the waters and trusted my purpose, fortune favored my boldness. I found a job as a schoolmaster in the City. And I also discovered a wondrous new fellowship with others like me: a band of freethinkers calling themselves the Robin Hood Society. We gathered at the east end tavern by that name.

Lights brighten. A sound of pub noise, laughter, voices, fiddle music. PETER smiles in remembrance and walks away from the table, raising his hand in greeting to persons unseen. He shakes hands, laughing as if he is with others. He stands behind his table and straightens as if he is younger. His voice is sharp and strong.

PETER *(to the audience, loudly, as if speaking to a crowd)*

Friends! We do ourselves and the cause of free thought honor by assembling here in the face of our enemy! *(applause)* In that regard let me welcome the spies sitting among us tonight. May my words cause you to learn other than the requirements of your stale mercenary profession! *(laughter)* And may tell your fat paymaster in Lambeth Palace that he too is welcome here! Although in truth I fear that even if he could lift his considerable weight from his plush cushions, the Bishop is as likely to accept my invitation as he is to give away all that he has to the poor and follow Christ!

Much laughter and applause as Peter smiles and pauses, then raises his hand for silence.

PETER

Brothers, let us address the matter at hand. Tonight, we Free Enquirers will apply our common reason to the fallacies we are expected to accept in blind faith from infancy. Take the proposition that an invisible God flooded the ancient land of Egypt with seven plagues to punish a slave-keeping Pharaoh. Well, my friends! Would that such heavenly retribution strike today's slave masters here in England! *(applause, cheers)* But God, it seems, is more tolerant of the crimes of slave owners and monarchs these days. We have had no rivers turn to blood here, although in truth such an event would undoubtedly improve the stagnant and effluent quality of the Thames! *(laughter)* Nor has a legion of frogs descended from the skies to plague our land. Of course, if such a miracle was done in France, the people there would have thought the plague a blessing! For then every household would enjoy a rich fricassee, without needing to go about frog-hunting. *(laughter)* It seems that what is done as evil to one people is in fact a delicious repast to another!

Much laughter and applause.

Lights subdued. PETER steps back and changes his demeanor to a thoughtful one. Pause. He seems to age again and speaks more quietly to the audience.

PETER *(smiling)*

It was a happy time. I was fulfilled. We met every Thursday in the Robin Hood and Little John public house on Butcher's Row. What a joy, how restorative for my hopes, to be in the company of others who saw through religion! Free men who esteemed reason as our chief weapon with which to fight the enemy!

PETER begins to pace excitedly and gesture with his hands.

PETER

Our Freethinkers society was composed of simple working men with a natural understanding of things: shop keepers, laborers, locksmiths. We were not the effete aristocrats of Voltaire's intellectual salons who muse over our Deistic principles from the safety of their parlors. We were serious men whose lives depended on one another. We debated everything, from the falsity of Biblical miracles to the price of bread and the great changes sweeping France and America. And we proclaimed to our neighbors what we thought and what we hoped for. We were what the government calls a seditious conspiracy.

PETER becomes angry, slamming his hand on the table angrily.

PETER

Seditious? <u>Us</u>? What is more of a threat to public safety than the Crown itself? In the summer of 1744 when I joined the Robin Hood Society, eighteen free thinking publications in London alone were seized and banned by the Attorney General. Printers were arrested, writers manacled and entombed in these stinking prisons, special gangs of plug uglies were hired off the wharves to break up our meetings and beat up our speakers. A great fear descended on the City, and many of us fled. But I was not one of them. I stood my ground. The danger only stiffened my resolve.

Lights brighten. PETER sits at the table, as if he is with another.

PETER *(urgently)*

What news, then, Andrew? *(pause, surprised)* No, not all of them! When? *(pause)* They are likely in Newgate. Then there is just the two of us left. *(pause, confused)* What are you saying, man? So, you are turning tail too, are you? Of all people, Andrew! I took you as stronger! *(pause, then angrily)* How absurd! I have no claim to martyrdom! We have a cause to win! *(pause as he listens, then throws up his hands in anger)* Fine! Abandon the fight in its hour of need! I will carry on alone if I must, you cowardly bastard!

PETER stands up quickly and strides angrily away from the table. He paces the cell then stands near the window with his head bowed as the lights are subdued. He looks at the audience.

PETER

Our Robin Hood society was raided out of existence. I moved endlessly about the East End like the hunted man I was. I was expelled from my teaching post when word of my lectures reached my employer. I lived on the charity of others and the meager earnings from my books and pamphlets. *(pause)* That was the time of the Forty-Five and Prince Charlie's revolt, and the Crown perceived Jacobite rebels under every bed. That was their justification for their tyranny. But what they did or did not do was not the issue. What mattered was what I did.

PETER gestures into the distance and the lights become very subdued. Peter looks about furtively as a clock strikes three.

PETER

The streets of Whitechapel in the deep of night. Only cutthroats, strumpets, and fools come here at this hour. But in these dank hovels my mission is more safeguarded than if I dallied in the broad, day-lit avenues of Mayfair. For here dwell the men and women who hear and celebrate my words.

PETER *lifts a long tract from the table and unrolls it proudly, smiling excitedly.*

PETER *(happily)*

And thus did I present to London's poor the first of my many writings. The ideas that had been confined to my sermons and public lectures now appeared everywhere like a mutinous mustard seed, coating the walls of Stepney and Whitechapel! Such bold defiance was my answer to tyranny! It was a spark aimed at enflaming the dull and subjugated thoughts of the wretched masses of London! Hear my words! *(He reads from the scroll.)* "If the scriptures be truth, then they will bear examination; if they do not withstand our God given reason, then let them go, for they come from elsewhere than heaven! The Great Inner Awakening that is sweeping our land and the American colonies is arising from the understanding that the truth of all things lies within us, and us alone. Even the rudest and most ruined soul can judge for himself the highest and lowest of matters. Then where does that undeniable truth leave the present rulers of our lands, our churches, our palaces, and our alleged government: the enrobed and titled knaves who claim to own the truth and the land, and who smite down any of us who challenge them?"

PETER pauses to catch his breath excitedly.

PETER

"Friends, is it not said that the first shall be last, and the last shall be first in the kingdom of heaven? As it is above, then so below. So believe this when I say that our unfettered conscience shall one day occupy the thrones and pulpits now held by unscrupulous and self-seeking men! Their high towers must and shall fall!"

PETER pauses in exaltation. He closes the scroll and stares reflectively at the audience.

PETER

My call was like the one from Galilee. It said, all things are made new. <u>All</u> things. And as with anything new, some rejoiced and others reviled. And still others struck back. (*PETER sighs and sits tiredly. A long pause as he begins to speak sadly*) Soon after my broadsheets appeared, special constables dispatched by Bishop Sherlock tore down my words. Any person caught reading them was arrested on the spot. But by then my writings had been read and cherished by many. Some unknown but loyal friends duplicated my tracts and posted them in other neighborhoods.

PETER perks up and smiles.

PETER

Without my doing, my name quickly became a byword in both great and humble circles. I was publicly blessed and cursed, as the great seed I had planted took root. And with every passing day as the tumult I created spread, my longing to be in the thick of the fight grew with what it fed on. I was like Martin Luther in his full stride.

PETER pauses.

PETER

I had finally found my purpose. And it was all that was left to me.

Lights down as he stares at the audience.

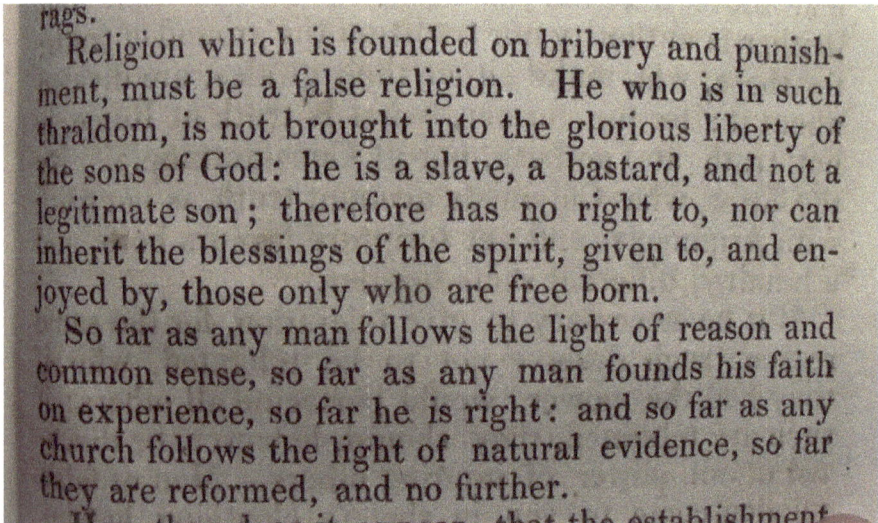

rags.
   Religion which is founded on bribery and punishment, must be a false religion. He who is in such thraldom, is not brought into the glorious liberty of the sons of God: he is a slave, a bastard, and not a legitimate son ; therefore has no right to, nor can inherit the blessings of the spirit, given to, and enjoyed by, those only who are free born.
   So far as any man follows the light of reason and common sense, so far as any man founds his faith on experience, so far he is right: and so far as any church follows the light of natural evidence, so far they are reformed, and no further.

SCENE THREE

A single light illuminates the image of a crown symbol above a judge's chair.

MALE VOICE *(upper class accent)*

State your name for the court.

FEMALE VOICE *(cockney accent)*

It is Elizabeth Annett, my Lord.

MALE

And for the record, are you appearing in court on your own recognizance and of your own free will?

FEMALE

Yes, my Lord.

MALE

Let the court record so indicate on this fifth day of March in the year of our Lord 1747. *(pause)* You are the legal wife of one Peter Annett, are you not?

FEMALE

Yes, I am.

MALE

I see you are the mother of an infant girl. Is Peter Annett her natural father?

FEMALE

Yes, my Lord. He is the father.

MALE

I see that you have made application to obtain a divorce from Master Annett.

FEMALE

Yes, sir.

MALE

You are aware, are you not, that divorce is not recognized nor is it lawful in our kingdom?

FEMALE

Yes, my Lord. But this is a special case about things besides our marriage. Well, that's what I was told at least by that Sheriff of yours.

MALE *(firmly)*

Strike that last remark from the record. *(pause)* Now tell the court any other matters involving your husband.

FEMALE *(nervously)*

Yes sir. He, my husband that is, well sir, Peter is involved in a, uh … *(pauses awkwardly, then speaks with difficulty)* in a suh, well sir, I think it's called something like …

MALE

Are you referring to sedition, madam? A conspiracy of that sort?

FEMALE

Yes, my Lord! A *(slowly)* … seditious conspiracy! That's the thing!

MALE

Against the Crown and the Church?

FEMALE

Yes sir! Peter blasphemes God out loud regular like!

MALE

And what else does your husband do, madam?

FEMALE

Well, he makes trouble for himself at those meetings he goes to.

MALE

With the so-called Robin Hood Society?

FEMALE

Yes, my Lord. That's the one.

MALE

you feel unsafe in your husband's company?

FEMALE

Yes sir, very much I do, sir!

MALE

For how long has your husband been engaged in these activities?

FEMALE *(hesitating, calculating)*

Well, I can't say for sure … I'll have to remember …

MALE

Madam, be assured that no fault will be ascribed to you for failure to report criminal activity. But you must be forthcoming with the court.

FEMALE *(relieved)*

Yes, my Lord, thank you, sir. *(pause)* Peter has always held strange ideas. He and I have been married just four years, sir, after he removed from Liverpool. In all that time he has never stopped from ridiculing holy scripture and cursing the Church. He rages about it constant like. And he gets together with others just like him …

MALE *(interrupting)*

Which others?

FEMALE

The Robin Hooders, sir, like I said. They have meetings at some pub.

MALE

To be sure. We are aware of them. Does your husband ever speak of his fellow plotters?

FEMALE

Oh, constant, sir, all the time. Least when I see him.

MALE

Do you not share the same home with him?

FEMALE

Well, not a lot no more, sir. He is away a lot.

MALE

You were describing the Robin Hood group. Continue.

FEMALE

Yes sir. He told me about them last time. Some of them were arrested and the rest are hiding.

MALE

Has he said where?

FEMALE

Not to me. Like I said, he don't keep my company much no more.

MALE

Are you aware of your husband's whereabouts today?

FEMALE

Oh, he could be anywhere about.

MALE *(sternly)*

I remind you that you are under oath, madam.

FEMALE

Yes sir. Honest, I don't know where he is right now.

Pause

MALE

I ask the court clerk to leave. *(pause)* Madam, what I have to say is solely between us. The Attorney General has instructed me to stay any charges brought against you in return for your assistance.

FEMALE

Yes sir.

MALE

Are you willing to give testimony regarding your husband before a special ecclesiastical court?

FEMALE

What's that, sir?

MALE

A church court, madam.

FEMALE

Oh yes, my Lord. Yes, I will.

MALE

That testimony will be provided to you and you will be expected to swear to its accuracy under oath. You must never discuss these matters with anyone. If you fail to abide by this arrangement, the full weight of the Crown will fall on you and your child.

FEMALE *(agitated)*

No, no, please sir. I agree to all that.

MALE

Then I require you to sign the statement before you. *(pause)* Good. And one final matter. From this moment forward you will assist our special constables in locating your husband and detaining him. The Crown will then favorably consider your request for a divorce.

FEMALE *(relieved)*

Oh, thank you, my Lord. Yes, I will do that, anything you ask.

MALE

You can go.

Lights go down.

SCENE FOUR

Lights up on PETER's cell. He is writing at his table. A sudden banging is heard as a rough male voice sounds from the outside.

VOICE

Annett! A letter for you!

PETER stands and hurries to stage left. He kneels as a slot opens and a folded piece of paper falls through. He walks slowly to the table and reads it. He tosses it away, looking despondent.

PETER *(to himself, shaking his head)*

Oh God help me, what a mistake.

He pauses, then looks up at audience and addresses them.

PETER

"For the lust of the flesh and of the eyes, and the pride of life, come not from God but from the master of this world." (pauses angrily) Where was that wisdom when I met her? Where was my common reason? Placed on a shelf to molder while I pursued her like a dog in rut until she was with child! Then what was there left but marriage? God curse me! What a price I have paid for my folly! *(pause)* Fifteen years!

PETER coughs heavily and slams the table. He turns and regards the letter lying crumpled on the floor, bends down and unfolds it. He turns to the audience and holds it up.

PETER *(angrily)*

These jabs Elizabeth still launches at me all these years later are aimed with evil design, and not by her alone. Make no mistake! Another hand guides her quill! These words are meant to stoke my despair and entomb my hopes completely!

PETER pauses, shaking with outrage.

PETER

Was it not enough that she who swore devotion to me before God led my enemies to my door? That she lied under oath about me in court and turned the key in this cell door? How could I have not perceived such corruption in the woman I loved? And now this!

PETER waves the letter. Then he reads from it.

PETER *(reciting)*

"Emily is a grown young woman now, but still she cries for you every night. If you would only repent from your sins, Peter, and admit your wrongs to the magistrate, you will be free to see her. I swear this to be true before God."

PETER pauses and looks at audience, outraged.

PETER

She swears it, does she? Just as she swore to be faithful to me alone until death! Then what am I to believe? That the Crown will annul its verdict and open this door if I renounce myself? That my daughter will still know me after so long and allow me to wipe away her tears? How more terrible than Christ's enticement in the desert is that offer to me, made by a more insidious devil that tempted our Lord!

*PETER crumbles again the letter and tosses it away angrily. He slumps in the chair and leans on the table. He begins to cough and then weep quietly and in despair. **He finally looks up.***

PETER *(somberly)*

I suppose that one can rage at Jezebel for only so long. Was not Hosea instructed by God to take back his harlot of a wife and continue to love her? Poor Elizabeth was always a timid soul. I was her rescuer, she told me once. I was the only man who had never harmed her. And in turn, I was the one who she could harm without fear of consequence.

PETER takes a long pause.

PETER

I thought my heart had been broken forever when my father died. But it was a mere pinprick compared to my anguish over my wee daughter Emily! *(gasps and sobs in anguish)* Ah, Emily! My mourning for that sweet child has no limits, even now! And how little solace from her memory has come from my vaunted reason! Once the mind diminishes and the heart takes hold, truly, there lies chaos! *(pause)* I once thought that I knew that. I <u>did</u> know that. But knowing is never enough.

PETER meditates briefly. He stares at his cell window. It is quiet outside. Peter turns to the audience.

PETER

Yesterday, after the food riots, I heard the burial carts come for the dead. How many people were killed by those cursed dragoons? Who knows? Who really cares, besides the victims' families? Like game to the slaughter, like pigs in the butcher's pen. Is that all we have become?

PETER returns to his chair and opens an imaginary book and pretends to read it. Pause.

PETER

One of the books my father forbade me to read was a work by a Swedish botanist named Linnaeus. It classified all the known plants and animals in our world into categories, including man. To Linnaeus, humanity is but one species in a long chain of animals operating according to natural laws. Those laws govern us as surely as they do donkeys and dandelions. How true!

PETER walks to the window and gestures out of it.

PETER

Look through those bars at the carnage in the streets and tell me if Man occupies a loftier elevation than the beasts of the field, as the tale of Genesis claims. It is nearly the year 1762 but still we are creatures driven by base impulses to feed and dominate and fornicate and fight for our survival against others. Reason is the God-given impulse to know and do better, but it fades like morning dew in the face of the day's furnace. I have relied on that elusive specter called reason. And yet, without that power to understand, to know things for ourselves …

PETER hesitates, pauses and looks at the audience.

PETER

"You are an obstinate and willful boy, Peter!" So said my father when he laid into me with his cane. But no amount of suffering ever made me doubt my thoughts. I never buckled to the beatings of either a father or a king. For the pearl of great price does not reside in the world. It lies no further than our own minds.

PETER smiles triumphantly and stands. He walks to the prison door and bangs it loudly.

PETER

Jailer! Where is my bundle? *(pause, as he bangs the door even harder)* I know you're there, you addler! I want the bundle you're keeping from me!

VOICE *(sounds roughly from outside)*

Quiet you or you won't get nuthin'!

PETER

My paper and my bundle! I want it promptly! It's my due and you know it!

VOICE *(coughing)*

Bugger off, you shite!

PETER kicks the door angrily. He calms and turns to the audience.

PETER

I suppose I pity my jailer. He is a crippled sailor whose legs were smashed by a French cannonball. He has worked in this cesspit for over twenty years and like me he is coughing out his life from consumption. He suffers worse than I. *(pause)* His name is Thomas Fairchild.

PETER paces thoughtfully to center stage and scratches his face. He looks at the audience.

PETER

Last year a third German George was crowned the king of England. This one is even more mad than your typical monarch. I read in one of the occasional news sheets they give me that this king forgot the name of his bride when he spoke his vows to her at their wedding. Truly.

PETER smiles and holds up his hands. Then he sobers.

PETER

It was rumored the new king would issue an amnesty for those of us imprisoned under the Blasphemy Act. But the Archbishop of Canterbury cut that down short shrift.

PETER pauses and looks wistful.

PETER

Poor Thomas my jailer broke the news to me. He fairly gloated at my misfortune, saying I deserved to stay locked up here my entire life. *(pause)* Do you not find it odd and terrible to see a beaten dog lick the hand of its master and defend it? But it is those curs like Thomas for whom I have fought. In them I have reposed my highest hopes that one day they will snap their chains once they own their thoughts and judge all things for themselves. *(pause, smiles)* It seems now, after so long, that this hope is sweeter to me than the kiss of a beloved and faithful wife.

He stares wistfully at the audience briefly, then returns to his writing table, looks at his papers and begins writing. Lights down.

SCENE FIVE

In the darkness, the image appears of PETER's collection of essays "The Free Enquirer". The voices of two elderly men are heard conversing: the SOLICITOR GENERAL and the BISHOP OF LONDON.

SOLICITOR

"Why cannot you judge for yourselves what is true?". (pause) I believe that is the offending passage, your Grace?

BISHOP *(agitated)*

One of many offenses, your Honor. But yes, that is the quotation. It sums up the cheek and presumptuousness of the man.

SOLICITOR

I assume you are referring to Reverend Annett? He was merely quoting our Lord Jesus. From the Gospel of St. Luke.

BISHOP *(angrily)*

Yes, and he worsens his crime by blasphemously perverting our Savior's words and their intent! He paints Christ as some kind of wild freethinker! He even denies our Lord's holy resurrection!

43

SOLICITOR

As do various Christian sects, your Grace, and we have not seen fit to prosecute them. Annett's writings are no more inflammatory than any of the other Deists, men like Toland and Woolston ...

BISHOP *(interrupting angrily)*

Both of whom were prosecuted for libeling our Lord and were jailed for years! Their guilt is Annett's! Their sentence should be his!

SOLICITOR

Annett has been duly judged and sentenced by our Court of King's Bench, Bishop. His year in Bridewell is nearly half served. Would you have me throw away the key to his cell?

BISHOP

I would do so in an instant if I occupied your position as Solicitor-General!

SOLICITOR

Then I thank God you do not! For it is the opinion of His Majesty's government that the best policy towards free thinkers and Deists is an inobtrusive and moderate suppression, lest we engender public sympathy for them.

BISHOP *(indignantly)*

Sympathy? For their kind? From who?

SOLICITOR

They have a following among many commoners. The Radicals have embraced them. John Wilkes refers to them in his newspaper …

BISHOP *(interrupts contemptuously)*

Bah! Atheistic traitors, all of them! What care we for their kind?

SOLICITOR

It is precisely their kind who are threatening the stability of the French king and our rule among our American colonists. I remind your Grace that we are at war with France and Spain. We cannot afford domestic strife. I suggest you look past your immediate interests to the broader political consequences …

BISHOP *(interrupting)*

Your Honor, I did not come here to discuss politics. Nor would I presume to instruct you in your duties as Solicitor-General, except to say it is my belief that you must make a more severe example of Peter Annett. As you know, His Excellency the Archbishop concurs with me and has impressed this fact on his Majesty.

SOLICITOR

But why Annett? He is an old man, impoverished and abandoned by his former colleagues.

BISHOP *(angrily)*

His rantings were responsible for the premature death of my predecessor, Thomas Sherlock! Annett's deistic filth was posted on the door of the Bishop's residence the day before his death from a stroke! There is no limit to Annett's depravity! He has deliberately incited an armed London mob against us! Surely that is sedition? A crime punishable by death!

SOLICITOR *(laconically)*

So says the law, at least. But consider as well, your Grace, that a man must be tried according to facts and evidence. We have no evidence that Annett posted the offending tract to which you refer. Nor has he been associated with any kind of armed mob. From all accounts, the man is a quiet, scholarly soul.

BISHOP *(agitated)*

Scholarly! You make him seem like a saint! *(pause, more soberly)* I see this is fruitless. You actually admire this villain! I have never understood you Whigs, nor will I attempt to.

SOLICITOR

You misjudge me, your Grace. Admiration does not imply acceptance. We imprisoned Annett because his Free Enquirer publication was found circulating as wall sheets among the common folk of Whitechapel and Stepney. His manner of appealing directly to the mob is unusual for Deists. And it is potentially dangerous, especially since his writings have also found their way to France and America. His sentence was issued with all of that in mind.

BISHOP

I'm afraid that's hardly comforting, sir, when the man will be released in a matter of months.

SOLICITOR

I am bound by the law, your Grace.

BISHOP *(accusingly)*

The law of man or of God? *(pause)* Your Honor, I am compelled to report our discussion to the Archbishop, who as you know has taken a keen interest in this matter. I am sorry I intruded on your valuable time.

SOLICITOR

Hardly an intrusion, Bishop. And please give pause. While I cannot overturn the court's decision or reopen his case, there are other means to satisfy your concerns.

BISHOP

I trust they will be effective.

SOLICITOR

If you consider denying an old man his livelihood an effective deterrent, your Grace, then yes. You need not worry. At Annett's age, after a year in Bridewell and with his life in ruins, the man will pose a threat to no-one. He will be unable to survive. We will ensure that.

BISHOP

The Archbishop will be most appreciative, sir. As will no doubt be His Majesty.

SOLICITOR

And of course, in return, our government will expect a grateful reciprocity from Lambeth, especially in these uncertain times.

BISHOP

That of course is a matter for the Archbishop. But I will certainly speak to him. *(pause, more subdued)* Sir, I am still at a loss concerning your admiration of this rascal Annett.

SOLICITOR

The man has a rare courage. And his thoughts are not uncommon, Bishop, even among royalty. Were you aware that our former Queen Caroline frequented free thinkers' salons? *(pause)* Judging matters for ourselves is not necessarily a subversive creed, your Grace. In fact, it is an Englishman's birthright. We cannot assume it to be wrong or sinful.

BISHOP

I advise you to tread carefully, sir. As you say, these are dangerous times.

Lights down.

SCENE SIX

The sound of a heavy door opening, shuffling steps, then the sound of a body falling to the floor and a man's moaning. Lights up on PETER lying face down on the floor of his cell. He slowly raises his head. His face is bloody and beaten. He crawls to the chair.

PETER *(weakly)*

Christ.

He pulls himself onto the chair and dabs his face with a towel, wincing with pain as he wipes away the blood with both hands. He looks at the blood on his hands and shakes his head. Then he looks at the audience and holds up his blood-stained hands.

PETER *(soberly)*

British justice. Or what passes for it. *(sighs, pauses)* He was a cold bastard, that judge who sentenced me, all high and mighty in his red robes. I asked him why he was giving a man in my condition six months at hard labor. (*imitating upper crust accent*) *"Of that you have none but yourself to blame, sir!". (pause, smiling)* I answered him that when I was released from prison his house would be the first one where I would post my next broadsheet. *(pause)* He added six months to my sentence.

PETER shrugs. He picks up his quill as if to write and then examines his inkpot and finds it empty.

PETER

Damn. *(He turns to the cell door).* Fairchild! Are you there? I need ink! *(pause)* Damn it, man!

PETER turns away and then remembers something. He reaches in his pants and extracts a pencil stub. He smiles, kisses it, and scribbles with it on paper, reciting slowly what he writes.

PETER

"My faithful readers will no doubt wonder what course this revived *Free Enquirer* shall chart once its author has escaped the dank recesses of Bridewell. *(He pauses and looks up)* Restrain your curiosity but a moment while I assure those of you who may doubt my continued fidelity to reason that I do not anticipate a Biblical miracle will free me from my prison, like some latter-day Paul or Silas. Forebear it for sudden blindness to strike down my jailer, or for a phantasmic being to appear and lead me out of this place! Let us leave such cruel and stupid make believe to our churchly adversaries."

PETER smiles and sits back. He turns to the audience.

PETER *(fervently)*

The mind and will strengthen even as the body fails. I must do more now than I have ever done! Every second matters!

PETER turns to his manuscript again and continues to scribble. Then he drops his pencil and stands facing the audience, wiping blood from his eyes.

PETER *(speaking as if to a crowd)*

Hear me! In these past few hours as the blows of my enemy fell upon me, a great scale fell from my eyes! I see how I have been like a blind man hunting vermin in a gutter rather than taking higher aim at the beast from which they spring!

PETER steps towards the audience with his arms open wide.

PETER *(urgently)*

Listen to me, all of you! This monster that we fight outlasts time and kingdoms! It seeks to enthrall mankind in my time as well as yours!

He pauses and crouches down close to the audience.

PETER *(quieter but impassioned)*

You see, for so long I have not perceived this thing. I have seen only its consequences in the men and women it makes stupid and then devours. For it cannot abide free, thinking people; only slaves. Because we are stronger than it when we stand in our natural reason and goodness. And so, through the ones it has birthed, the kings and popes and wealthy of this world, it subjugates men's minds so we will do its bidding, against all reason: to war against each other and ruin ourselves for its malignant profit. This thing feeds off our sorrows and our suffering.

PETER stares at the audience and sits back on the stage. Pause.

PETER *(conversationally)*

How do I know this? How can I prove this to you, as I must as a reasonable man? The proof is all around you and within you. It is freely visible to you in all its hideousness once you recover your God-given minds. But the laws of Church and State prohibit such liberty and such insight. They will strike you down if you seek it. And in your fear of that outcome, they have you as manacled as if you were here with me in this cursed place.

PETER sighs and shakes his head.

PETER *(regretfully)*

Ah, if only I had known sooner! *(shouting angrily)* Christ! All those wasted years! All my rhetorical tilting at windmills, jousting with the phantasms conjured by this thing to distract me from the truth! And yet how does one learn except through such defeat? *(pause)* Or am I lying to myself? Have I ruined my chance to strike even one decisive blow at the head and the heart of this monster?

PETER stares reflectively at the audience. His face becomes drawn and despairing.

PETER

How I tremble for what is to come. While this thing lives, its power will only grow, fed by new machinery and the sweated labor of millions. I have seen the future in the mills of Lancashire where children as young as four sweat out their short, pathetic lives to pile up the wealth of the aristocrats of finance who rule our Empire! The legions of black slaves on the Liverpool docks are but a precursor to the bondage that awaits mankind. And the strongest chains will be those that encircle men's minds. *(pause)* Unless.

Pause as PETER recovers his resolve.

PETER *(firmly)*

Unless! Unless we put away the childish thoughts that keep us suckled to this beast. Unless we use our freed minds to smash every chain that makes one man to rule over and profit off another. Unless every gilded throne is thrown onto the trash heap and each man knows the other to be his equal. Unless we finally judge all things for ourselves.

PETER stares at the audience, then smiles.

The truth does set us free. Even in this place. *(He gestures to his cell).* Even in that place. *(He gestures to the audience).* But what will you do with the truth? And what will you do now? *(pause, to himself)* What shall I do?

PETER pauses and then stands slowly. He walks slowly to the table and sits again. He looks at the paper on which he wrote. He touches it and looks at the audience. Then he turns to the page and begins writing again. Lights down.

THE
FREE ENQUIRER.

No. 6.]　　　　　SATURDAY.　　　[Nov. 21, 1761.

The prosecution of the Review of the Life and Doctrines of Moses is postponed to our next Paper, to allow the publication of the following Epistles, with which we have been favoured; and which we are solicitous to show our ingenious Correspondents we do not neglect.

REFLECTIONS ON THE RIGHT OF PRIVATE JUDGMENT.

YEA, "and why even of yourselves judge ye not that which is right?" Luke xii. 57. Why must you be told every thing? You are all taught of God, the nature and reason of things is the voice of God. Honestly use the sense he has given you; he requires no more of you, but the improvement of your own abilities; they are the talents he has given you, the interest you gain will be your own. But by wrapping your talent up in a napkin, and laying it by from a principle of fear! you insult your maker in the act, and ruin youreslf in the event.

"Wherefore then judge ye not of yourselves that which is right?" Why are not those who fancy themselves to be free-willers, and free-actors, free to judge aright of principles that are proposed to their judgment? but because they are bred up in, and habituated to, the belief of what they venerate as sacred truths, or fear to disbelieve because of invisible bugbears, and of feeling the most exquisite sensible torments, when they have lost all feeling, and every other sense. Are these men free? Are not these fetters that enslave them? And these tyrannical ter-

SCENE SEVEN

Pictures of Peter and London's east end appear. A Narrator's voice is heard.

NARRATOR

Peter Annett spent another year in Bridewell Prison. By the time he emerged in 1763, his already fragile health was destroyed. But though his body was in ruins, his mind was as alert and active as ever. Peter was resolved to re-publish his *Free Enquirer* newspaper and once more take the fight to the steps of the church and his archenemy, the Bishop of London.

But circumstance and both his friends and adversaries had other plans. The circle of freethinkers he had known had vanished. So too had the once-passionate support for his cause among the handful of his supporters from his early days. They all shunned Peter as if he carried leprosy. Such is the fate of men targeted by Church and State.

Undeterred, Peter sought out the familiar east end streets where he had once been so well received, but even there all the doors were closed to him. No printer dared to produce The Free Enquirer. Everywhere he went he was followed and harassed. The Bishop had Peter locked up as tightly as when he languished in Bridewell.

Eventually, as impoverished and alone as ever, Peter settled in a small room in St. George's Gardens. From there he returned to teaching a few young students. But soon his frank criticism of the Bible alarmed their parents and his school collapsed. Then his attempt to produce a grammar book for children also failed when the publisher insisted that he employ a pseudonym rather than the "infamous" name Annett. For Peter refused to deny his identity.

Through every new defeat, the old man continued to write his reflections and plan to confront his enemies in campaigns that never happened. But his vision burned as strong as ever.

In 1768, the year before he died, Peter Annett struggled to publish his final work: a compendium of his writings he entitled, *"A Collection of the Tracts of a Certain Free Enquirer, Noted for His Sufferings for His Opinions."* It is believed this book saw the light of day, but like most of his works, no copy of it survived. The only evidence of Peter's publications emerged sixty years later, when in 1826 a radical London printer named Richard Carlile published the nine issues of *The Free Enquirer* that had sent Peter to prison.

We can only imagine the events surrounding Peter's final days. The substance of the man is evident and requires no speculation.

Lights down.

SCENE EIGHT

Lights up on a room similar to Peter's Bridewell prison cell, minus the bars on the window, which harbors some thin curtains. A rocking chair sits in a corner, opposite to a long table on which is strewn papers and books. A kitchen cupboard is in another corner.

PETER ANNETT shuffles in from stage right. His hair is completely white and long but less scraggly. He walks slowly with a cane with a stooped, painful posture. He is bespectacled and is dressed in a robe and slippers. Mumbling to himself as he rummages through books and papers, finally cursing in frustration and tossing a book to one side. He holds up a book and removes a piece of paper.

PETER

There you are. Thought you'd hide on me again, did you?

PETER squints at the paper and is mumbling something when a sharp rap comes from his door. PETER ignores it until the rapping becomes louder.

PETER *(calling out without looking up)*

Be gone with you! Do you hear me?

As the knocking continues, PETER walks to the rocking chair and sits, reading the paper and book, oblivious to the sound.

After a few moments, a young man in his twenties enters the room from stage right: SAMUEL WENTWORTH. He is clean-shaven and well dressed.

SAMUEL

Excuse me, sir. Pardon my intrusion. *(PETER continues to read and ignore him).* Uh, excuse me, but are you Peter Annett. *(pause)* Sir?

After a pause, PETER looks up, notices SAMUEL and looks shocked.

PETER *(alarmed)*

Christ! Who in hell are you?

SAMUEL

Samuel Wentworth, sir. *(He extends his hand and PETER merely frowns angrily at him)* I am sorry for this intrusion …

PETER *(snapping)*

Then why are you here if you're sorry?

SAMUEL

Oh! Well it's just an expression. I'm sorry, I mean.

PETER

Say what you mean then, boy!

SAMUEL *(nervously)*

A mutual friend suggested I speak to you.

PETER

I have no friends! Who are you babbling about?

SAMUEL

Andrew Wheatley, sir. He says you were acquainted at the Robin Hood Inn.

PETER *(interrupting, outraged)*

Wheatley? That shit festooned, white-livered dung heap has no business calling himself my friend! Not when he abandoned me and our cause like some skittish schoolgirl!

SAMUEL looks down nervously and uncertain.

PETER *(accusingly)*

What did he do, send you here to spy on me? Is he working for that whoring sodomite Bishop Terrick?

SAMUEL *(anxiously)*

No, no, I am here on my own volition, sir. Believe me! I am a great admirer of your work!

PETER *(scowling)*

Bah! Be gone with you!

PETER returns to his reading. SAMUEL stares at him uncertainly, then walks to the table and notices the table's contents. He studies some of the papers. Pause.

SAMUEL

Are these some of your recent writings, sir?

PETER looks up with the same scowl but then his expression turns more benign as he sees SAMUEL's interest.

PETER

You are not a spy, then?

SAMUEL

No sir! I am a Deist, like you! I have read everything you've written along with Thomas Woolston and John Toland and …

PETER *(angrily)*

Woolston and Toland! Don't you go citing those charlatans to me, boy! They hadn't the courage of their own convictions and they suffered nothing for them! It fell to me to carry that burden, and to me alone! Do you comprehend?

SAMUEL nods deferentially. They stare at each other. PETER finally softens.

PETER

To answer you, I have written nothing in more than a year.

SAMUEL

May I ask why?

PETER *(shaking his head)*

Toland and Woolston indeed! Good God!

PETER returns to his book.

SAMUEL

But sir, why are you no longer writing?

PETER *(without looking up)*

Ask yourself the same question in fifty years, boy. Then perhaps you will have your answer. But I doubt it.

SAMUEL looks disappointed. He gazes about the room.

Finally, SAMUEL stands and faces PETER.

SAMUEL

Sir, if it is your wish, I will bid you adieu. But please be assured that it would be my honor to assist you however I can. Your work is important and it must continue. Your story must be told. Perhaps I could be your scribe and help you accomplish that.

PETER looks up and studies SAMUEL more carefully. He softens again and sighs. He removes his glasses and rubs his eyes tiredly. Then he looks at SAMUEL again.

PETER *(quietly)*

You must forgive me. Samuel is it? *(SAMUEL nods)* I am seventy-four years old and an angry old curmudgeon. Please.

PETER gestures to the chair. SAMUEL sits back down.

PETER *(smiles gently)*

Good. Now let me tell you something. I will only say it this one time. Someone with your offer should have come to me ten years ago. The tip of my quill is worn to nothing, my young friend. I am spent. That is the hard case of it.

SAMUEL

Then let me carry the burden for you. All you need do is recite.

PETER *(sadly)*

I could have, once, when I was certain. But I am no longer.

SAMUEL

Certain? Concerning what?

PETER looks at SAMUEL. He closes his eyes and shakes his head.

SAMUEL

You mean about your beliefs? About reason?

PETER *(eyes still closed)*

It is more, much more than that. (*PETER opens his eyes and sits back in his rocking chair, staring at SAMUEL.*) There is no cure for what we face, son. Not even reason can see its way through it.

SAMUEL stares at him in confusion.

PETER

Do not try to understand, Samuel. It cannot be understood. Nor can it be written. Why else has my quill been still? (*SAMUEL shakes his head and looks despondent.*) I see that my words disappoint you; perhaps as much as they disappoint me.

Pause as they stare at each other in silence.

SAMUEL

Will you at least allow me to re-issue the various numbers of your *Free Enquirer*?

PETER gestures to the kitchen cupboard.

PETER

You will find them in there. I would be obliged. I have no heirs.

SAMUEL

No children?

PETER stares at him sadly in silence, then looks away. Pause.

SAMUEL

You said there is no cure for what we face. What is that? I mean, the thing we face.

PETER *(smirking)*

The thing, indeed.

PETER stands slowly and wearily and motions to his cane, which stands against the table. SAMUEL fetches it for him. He hobbles to the cupboard and removes a leather bag. He hands it to SAMUEL and then gestures to it.

PETER

It is all there. The only words I have penned this past year. And there is more.

PETER sits heavily on a chair. He looks at SAMUEL thoughtfully.

PETER

We are not God-fearing men, are we, Samuel?

SAMUEL *(confused)*

I am uncertain of your meaning.

PETER

God is the great Unknowable, never perceived directly but only derivatively in our capacity to reason. It is the slice of divinity within each of us. Correct?

SAMUEL

Aye, sir. That is an axiomatic principle of our Deism.

PETER

Does that satisfy you? (*SAMUEL stares at him, looking even more confused.*) Does it feed the longings of your heart or explain this sorry mess we wrongly call civilization?

SAMUEL

It isn't meant to. We must create solace and understanding.

PETER

Through reason. Through right action arising therefrom.

SAMUEL

Why, of course. As you yourself have written so often.

PETER *(nodding reflectively)*

Aye, as I have written. As I believed. *(pause)* *"The fear of God is the beginning of wisdom."* *(pause)* How do you interpret that passage from the Proverbs, Samuel?

SAMUEL *(curtly)*

It is mere priestcraft, sir. One cannot find wisdom through fear.

He takes a seat next to PETER.

PETER

You misunderstand the Biblical meaning of the word "fear". The Hebrew term is "yarah". It refers not to terror, but reverence. To revere and respect God is wisdom. *(pause, smiles)* We Deists are hardly known for that quality.

SAMUEL

What quality?

PETER

Reverence.

Pause.

SAMUEL

Forgive me, but your point eludes me.

PETER nods. Pause.

PETER

My father accused me of holding nothing to be sacred. He was correct, Samuel. But for all my assumed wisdom, my insistence that all things must be proven before they can be honored, was I not but mirroring the mind of the monster all about me? This thing England is becoming? And through England, the entire world? A world where nothing will be revered because all things will be violated and cheapened, beginning with man himself.

PETER holds up a hand to his face and closes his eyes. He shakes his head sadly. SAMUEL stares at him with concern.

SAMUEL

You told me there is no cure for what we face. Is it that to which you refer? This barren future of which you speak?

Long pause as PETER stares at him sadly. He gestures to the leather bag SAMUEL holds.

PETER

Besides my writing, you will find in there correspondence. One of the letters comes from an impoverished laborer in Birmingham. A man named Thomas Watkins. He had just buried his youngest child: a three-year-old girl named Rebecca. *(pause, gravely)* I suggest you read it. Especially the manner of Rebecca's death.

PETER gestures to the leather bag. SAMUEL gives it to him and PETER sorts through it and removes and hands to SAMUEL a crumpled single page. SAMUEL reads it. He looks increasingly confused and finally horrified. He looks at PETER wide-eyed.

SAMUEL

This cannot be!

PETER *(holding up the bag)*

It is attested by others. Their statements are all here.

SAMUEL *(shocked, gasping)*

It is monstrous!

PETER

It is the way of things there. And in Manchester and Liverpool and wherever the poor are corralled like cattle awaiting slaughter. Their children are traded among the rich like so many choice morsels, and then disposed of like poor little Rebecca Watkins. So, I ask you, Samuel: has the future not arrived? *(pause)* What is reason's answer to this senseless slaughter?

SAMUEL *(angered)*

It must be stopped, of course!

PETER

And who will stop it, Samuel? The mill owners, who profit off the trade? The aristocrats and their relatives in government, who are served by it? Could Thomas Watkins save his own child? It is like expecting a mouse to undo the cat that hunts his kind.

SAMUEL

You have no hope, then. No faith in people.

PETER *(chucking ironically)*

Faith? Truly an odd word for a Deist to utter! Come down to earth, Samuel. You hear not despair from me. I speak from a lifetime of labor. I struggled for years to arouse the people of the east end to their mental captivity to an enslaving religion.

SAMUEL

Aye, of course. And you paid a stiff price for it.

PETER *(quickly)*

One caused by my own stubborn refusal to perceive the nature of our enemy; by my presumption that our slavery is simply a matter of harboring the wrong ideas or of not applying reason properly. *(pause)* The brutal truth, Samuel, is that reason is stillborn in mankind, for it is trampled to dust before it can even attempt to expel evil from its gilded throne and counting house.

SAMUEL smiles.

PETER

Are my words amusing?

SAMUEL

Nay, sir.

PETER

Then what amuses you?

SAMUEL

I was recalling when you wrote that one cannot toss a stone at the Church of England without striking the Crown. It is small wonder you are feared at Lambeth and Westminster alike.

PETER

It has always been so, Samuel. Their agents still linger hereabout. No doubt you were observed by them this day.

SAMUEL looks surprised, then troubled and uncertain.

PETER *(smiling ironically)*

Now, do you still wish to stop their abominations?

SAMUEL *(offended, irritated)*

What just man would not?

PETER

I am speaking of you, Samuel. Everything bears a price. The state has a long memory and an unforgiving nature towards men like us. *(pause)* But what of my legacy? Does your offer remain?

SAMUEL *(passionately)*

You mean regarding your *Free Enquirer*? Of course! I will not rest until they are reissued and known to every Englishman!

PETER looks at him appreciatively. He nods his thanks with a smile.

PETER *(cheerily)*

Well then, Master Wentworth! It appears that some part of me may yet survive. Pray that it falls on good soil.

The two men smile at each other.

Lights down.

Last known residence of Peter Annett, St. George's Gardens, London

SCENE NINE

Lights up on a London printing shop owned by RICHARD CARLILE. He is a middle-aged, rotund, and amiable man. He stands behind a counter facing a well-dressed old man: SAMUEL WENTWORTH. It is the year 1826, over a half century after he spoke with PETER.

CARLILE

The galley proofs are completed, Mister Wentworth, sir. They are hanging in my shop if you would care to examine them.

SAMUEL

My deepest thanks are owed you, Mister Carlisle. It is a dream finally realized.

CARLILE

I understand you were personally acquainted with the author.

SAMUEL

Aye, sir. I had that honor when I was a mere lad.

CARLILE

I could find no literary reference to Peter Annett except one attributed to Oliver Goldsmith, in which he condemns him for his attacks on scripture and on certain church figures.

SAMUEL *(smiling)*

Oh aye, Peter took great delight in antagonizing Bishops. He was not one to trim his sails to match the prevailing winds.

CARLILE *(nodding)*

And it is that quality of his character that our readers will find most compelling. As you know, we cater to the City's radical reading rooms and their sponsors.

SAMUEL

That is precisely why I chose your printshop, Mister Carlile.

CARLILE

A pity that such establishments were not common in Peter's time. Men like him were solitary voices in the wilderness.

SAMUEL

Well sir, I fear the political climate is hardly improved these days.

CARLILE

Granted. The news from Lancashire is grim indeed.

SAMUEL

Is there an estimate of the number shot dead?

CARLILE

At least a dozen of the poor souls. Another two hundred of the loom breakers were arrested. Transportation for the lot of them is likely. *(pause)* A high price to pay to protect their livelihoods.

SAMUEL

They call themselves Luddites, is the rumor.

CARLILE *(smiling)*

I warrant if your Peter Annett were alive, he would have something to say about it, as the Church of England is the chief shareholder in that infernal company that brought in the power looms.

SAMUEL *(nodding)*

Peter seemed to blow a single Deist note, but his concerns were many. He spoke against the slave trade and championed the rights of the fairer sex. He appealed to women as natural freethinkers.

CARLILE *(glancing at his pocket watch)*

I am mindful of the hour, Mister Wentworth. Would you care to see the proofs of your friend's *Free Enquirer*?

SAMUEL *(smiling)*

That is not necessary, sir. I trust you have matters well in hand.

CARLILE

The first print run will be this Friday. *(pause)* Oh, and I took the liberty of adding this footnote to the end of his final chapter.

CARLILE hands him a page, which SAMUEL reads.

SAMUEL *(emotionally, wiping away a tear)*

It is a fitting tribute to Peter. My thanks, sir.

CARLILE *(nodding)*

I pray our small effort will honor the man and his ideas. *(pause)* Were you with him at his end?

SAMUEL *(somberly)*

Sadly, I was not. Circumstances separated us. I had my own troubles with which to contend. *(pause)* He was buried in Potter's Field in Southwark. An anonymous grave without even a marker. *(pause)* Perhaps that was fitting. Peter told me once that truth has been banished to a pauper's grave.

CARLILE

Perhaps now the dead will arise, Mister Wentworth.

SAMUEL smiles.

SAMUEL *(reciting)*

"At the trumpet of reason, the dead shall be raised. Before that bar, all shall come to judgement."

CARLILE

His words?

SAMUEL nods.

SAMUEL

His cure, Mister Carlile. His answer to the monster.

The two men smile and shake hands. Lights down.

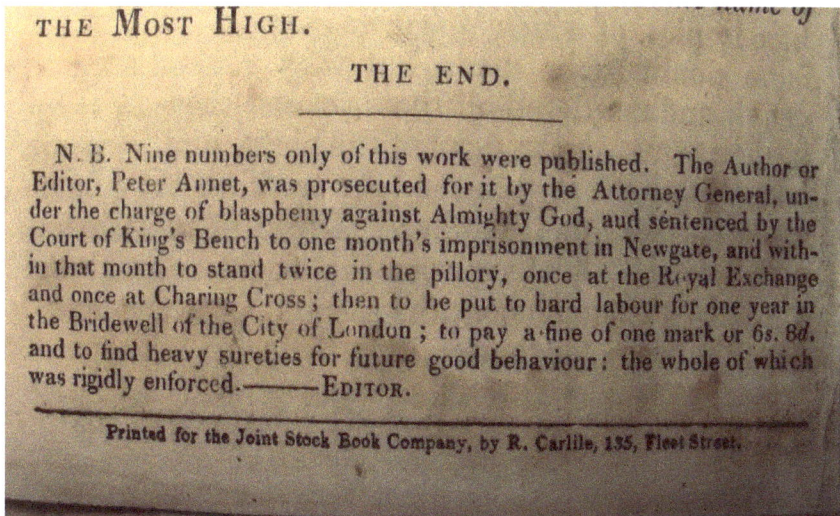

THE MOST HIGH.

THE END.

N. B. Nine numbers only of this work were published. The Author or Editor, Peter Annet, was prosecuted for it by the Attorney General, under the charge of blasphemy against Almighty God, and sentenced by the Court of King's Bench to one month's imprisonment in Newgate, and within that month to stand twice in the pillory, once at the Royal Exchange and once at Charing Cross; then to be put to hard labour for one year in the Bridewell of the City of London; to pay a fine of one mark or 6s. 8d. and to find heavy sureties for future good behaviour: the whole of which was rigidly enforced.———EDITOR.

Printed for the Joint Stock Book Company, by R. Carlile, 135, Fleet Street.

Postscript

I first encountered my ancestor Peter Annett over forty years ago in an antiquarian bookshop in Vancouver. How one of the few surviving copies of his *Free Enquirer* ended up there is anyone's guess. Nobody in our family had ever heard of Peter, except my father Bill.

"Voltaire collaborated with him and the church hated him, which is two strokes in his favor," Dad explained. "They locked him away when he was seventy for pissing off some Bishop. Now you know where you get it from, Kev."

Over the years since then, I have carried the fragile pages of the *Free Enquirer* with me as both an inspiration and a reminder. Its message and Peter's life are especially important nowadays, as a new tyranny descends on our liberties and our thinking. The Thing that Peter refers to in my script is as alive and voracious as ever. But so too is the eternal flame of human consciousness and conscience - and the memory of valiant freethinkers like Peter.

More than one of my associates have suggested that I could be the reincarnation of the old London firebrand, since our manner, our enemies, and our campaigns are so similar. Whether I am or not, the result is the same. The struggle continues.

Beyond the obvious parallels in our lives, Peter and I share an even deeper affinity that I tried to illustrate in this play: namely, what it means to be an exiled pariah in our own country and how we endure the destruction of our family, livelihood, and freedom by Church and State. The courage to persist against such enormous odds boils down to will, and a selfless commitment to a purpose greater than ourselves. That is part of the secret of our example.

At the end of the day, we need not fear. For we have it within ourselves the power to create the world anew. Or, as Peter put it in his first *Free Enquirer* issue that paved his way to jail and glory,

"The beauty of true understanding is more durable than what age withers and more radiant than what circumstance destroys. Wisdom and goodness are the attributes of divine nature and the birthright of every free man and woman."

Kevin Annett

About the Author

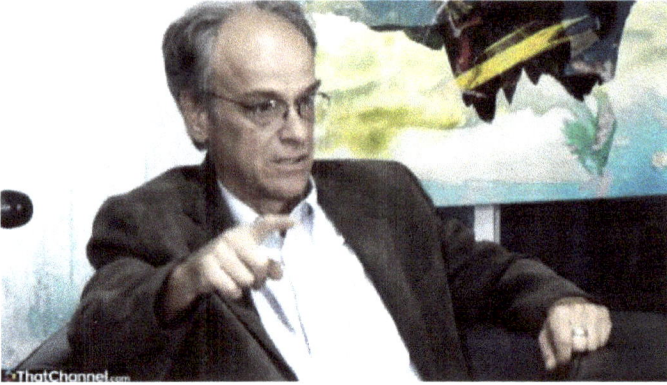

Kevin Annett is a former clergyman who has led the campaign to expose and prosecute Christian genocide in Canada and the world. A prolific writer, activist, and human rights figure, Kevin forced Canada's historic admission of its "Indian Residential Schools" crimes in 2008 and helped depose Pope Benedict in a common law court trial during 2013.

Despite being blacklisted and censored for many years, Kevin is the author of twenty-five books and two plays, and has produced several award-winning documentary films. He has twice been nominated for the Nobel Peace Prize and the Order of Canada.

Kevin's websites are www.murderbydecree.com and www.republicofkanata.org .

He can be contacted at angelfire101@protonmail.com .